To
Parents

Thank you for choosing our *Preschool Fun Story Activities* as your child's learning companion.

To maximize your child's experience with *Preschool Fun Story Activities*, it is vital that you provide a supportive environment in which your child can enjoy doing the activities. Here are some suggestions for you to help your child:

- Children feel a sense of achievement when they try new things and can complete them, so help your child finish whatever tasks he or she starts. Remember to give your child support whenever necessary, but refrain from taking over the task completely.

- Take the time to work with your child. Don't rush them through the activities because children need time to feel engaged with what they are doing.

- Always give encouragement. Positive reinforcement encourages children to learn and sustains their interest in learning. Look for achievements to praise and acknowledge your child's progress whenever possible.

- Nurture your child's creativity. Encourage your child to ask questions, try different ways, and engage him or her in spin-off activities that you may come up with.

With your involvement and encouragement, we are sure that your child will find working through *Preschool Fun Story Activities* a fun and rewarding experience.

Contents

Sorting Fun

Our Goodies

Cooking with Mother Duck

Stickers

Board Game

Sorting Fun

Come over here, Puppy! Watch
how I put my things.

Where do I put my toy car?

I put it in the toy box, with the balls and the robots.

Where do I put my shorts?

I put them in the drawer, with my T-shirts and socks.

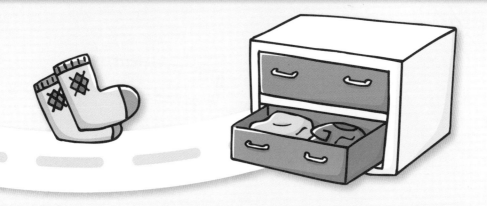

Where do I put this pencil?

I put it on my **desk**, with the
ruler and the eraser.

Where do I put this storybook?

I put it on the shelf, with the comics and the notebooks.

I put it in my **piggy bank**, with the pennies and the nickels.

Where do I put this cup?

I put it in the cupboard, with the bowls and the dishes.

Where do I put the milk?

I put it in the fridge, with the eggs and the cheese.

Where do I put the ice cream?

Where do I put you, Puppy?

I put you in your **bed**, with Kelly Cat and Benny Bunny.

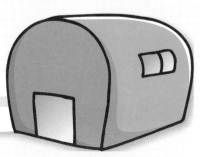

Look, Puppy! Look!
Everything is in the right
place where it belongs!

30

Activities

Color the paths.

Cut and paste.

hree
y dogs

family

apple

Flowers

Fun Time

Billy Bear

Draw lines to put the pencils on the desk.

Paste the coin stickers.

1¢

5¢

25¢

Trace the lines.

Paste the stickers.

Trace the lines. Then paste the stickers.

Cut and paste.

Our Goodies

Millie and Billy have lots of goodies.

2 two

Look at our brownies!
One brownie, two brownies...
We have **two** brownies!

3 three

Look at our cookies!
One, two, three...
We have **three** cookies!

Look at our carrots!
One, two, three, four...
We have **four** carrots!

4 four

5 five

Look at our apples!
One, two, three, four, five...
We have **five** apples!

Look at our bananas!

6 six

One, two, three, four, five, six...
We have **six** bananas!

One, two, three, four, five, six, seven...
We have **seven** cherries!

Look at our lollipops!

9 nine

Look at our jelly beans!

10 ten

One, two, three, four, five, six, seven, eight, nine, ten... We have **ten** jelly beans!

Let's count the goodies
with Millie and Billy.

1 one

2 two

5 five

8 eight

MILLIE and BILLY

3 three
4 four
6 six
7 seven
9 nine
10 ten

Activities

Color the paths.

one

2

2 two

Color the three cookies.

3 three

Trace the lines.

4
four

Paste the face stickers.

5 five

Circle the six bananas.

6 six

7
seven

8
eight

Circle the seven birds and color the eight kids.

Color the nine stripes.

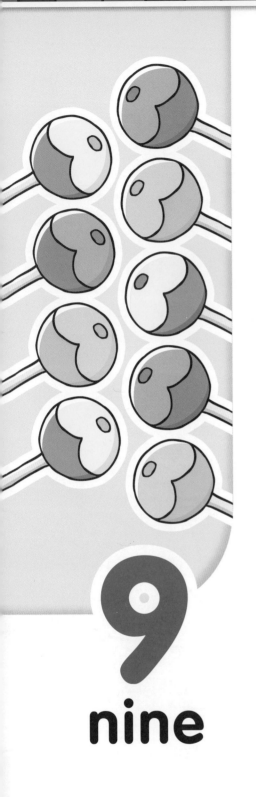

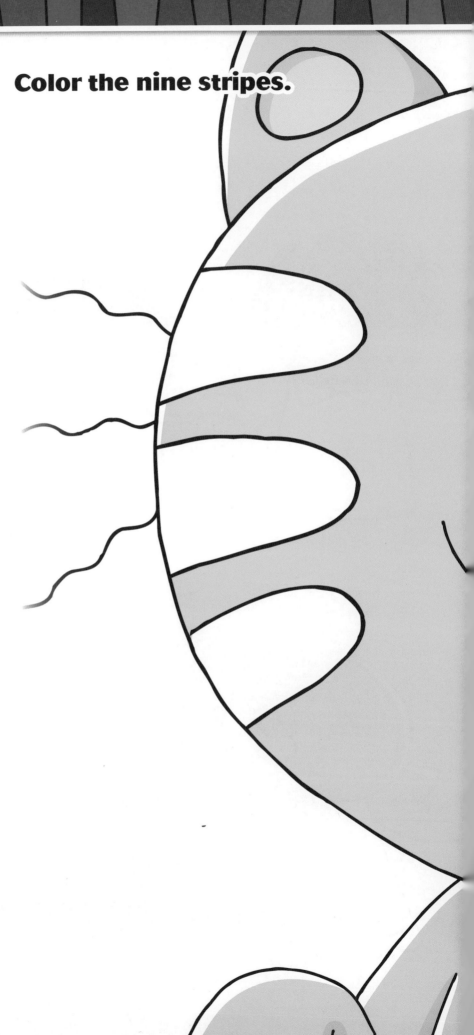

9
nine

Color the ten balls.

10
ten

Cooking with Mother Duck

Mother Duck loves to cook.

What's that on your apron, Mom?

Numbers

Write

Follow these steps to make this snack.

3

Counting

Quack! Quack! We need two plates.

Which one would you like?

3

Quack! Quack! May I have the green one, please?

Colors

Sizes

Quack! Quack! Thanks, Mom, but may I have a bigger one, please?

Quack! Quack! Now let me put a cracker on the plate.

Which shape do you like?

A square one, please.

Shapes

Quack! Quack! Let me put ice cream on the cracker.

Counting

1   2

104

Pattern

Strawberry, blueberry, strawberry, blueberry...

Quack! Quack! We need two spoons.

One for you and one for me.

Thanks, Mom!

One to One

Likely

Quack! Quack! Let's eat now or the ice cream will melt.

Not Likely

This is yummy. It cheers my tummy...Quack! Quack!

Activities

Circle the things with numbers.

Numbers

Say the numbers. Then cut and paste.

one

Follow the steps to draw.

1

2

3

Steps

Color.

3 Colors

4 Colors

Sizes

Trace and color.

Shapes

Pattern

Paste the sticker to complete the path.

HOME

Paste the stickers.

One to
One

Likely

Not Likely

Color the correct path to see how the doll looks after being washed.